Peace in a Child's Soul

Children's Meditation

Peace in a Child's Soul

Children's Meditation

Peter Lyons

Little Stars Little Moon
Portland, Oregon

Copyrighted © 2011 by Peter Lyons

All rights reserved.
Printed in the USA

ISBN 978-1-893075-41-2
Library of Congress Number: 2011921445

Cover Ethan Firpo
Illustrations by Suzanne Deakins
Book Design Spirit Press, LLC

This book may not be reproduced by electronic or any other means which exist now or may yet be developed, without permission of Spirit Press, except in the case of brief quotations embodied in critical articles and reviews.

Little Stars Little Moon
an imprint of
Spirit Press
www.littlestarslittlemoon.com
Portland, Oregon

Dedication

For all of the children; those yet to be born and the child we carry within. To enter heaven, return home, the land of milk and honey we must be as children, innocent and knowing all life is connected. Children know this as does our child within.

My Blue Hand Painting of Big Water
January 2011, Eildon Gabriel Wilkerson, age 4 years

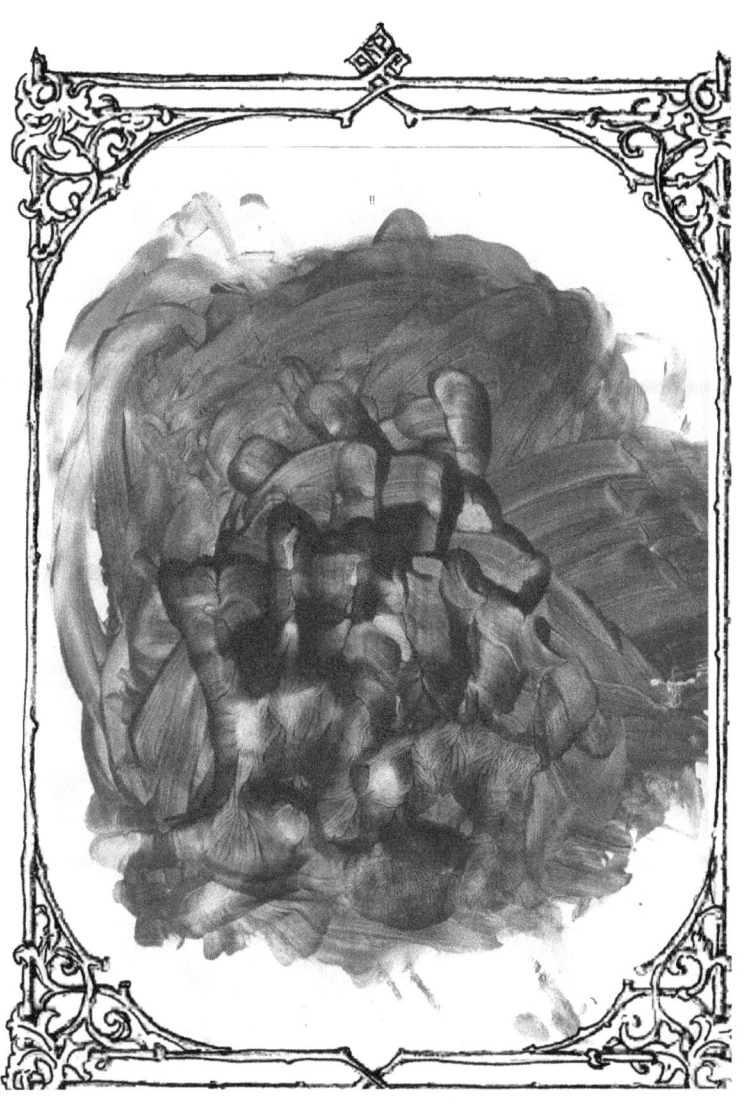

This is About Fire That is Very Hot
February 2011, Eildon Gabriel Wilkerson, age 4 years

Peace In a Child's Mind

We can go to almost any place
Be it under sea or outer space.
No there's nothing much we've yet to find
'Cept the peace of a child's mind

They can mesmerize and hypnotise
With how they see through their clear eyes
And no complicated guise of ours
Stops the peace of a child's mind

Yet we still impose ideals and dreams
On them, like we're the ones supreme,
And wonder why our life's extremes
Stills this peace in our own mind

Could it be they know more than we,
With their world built simplistically
There's no deceit or mystery
In the peace called a child's mind.

Introduction

While editing my original work, On the Light Path, A Psychic's Journey, it became quite clear that I had written more than could be chewed in one book. Large chunks had to be removed in order to make the book readable. One of the sections we had to sacrifice was the section relating to a specific meditation for children.

After the Light Path was safely in the hands of my publisher, I set about looking at what I could do with the children's meditation section, as a separate entity. It struck me, as I worked on what direction to take this publication, that we are all children deep within.

The part of us that we don't see in the mirror, the voice we don't hear on a recording device, the personality only we know of ourselves, that is our soul, and that is the child I refer to. The contented, childish, simply and easily entertained, with the least amount of external entertaining devices, that is the child like soul within.

So with this in mind I have intended this book for all children, whether they are the little people we care for in our lives, or the little person deep within us all. I have followed the same format as I did with Light Path, by incorporating anecdotal accounts as well as personal accounts, along with information passed on to me by my wonderful Guidance Team.

I have also continued the practice of incorporating the words from songs or poems I have written previously, appropriate to the particular chapter. I hope it is as enjoyable for you to read, as it was pleasurable for me to write.

The soul is so apparent in our children. Our job as parents is to nuture, protect, and help the child find peace. Nothing is more fundamental to a peaceful child then quiet time where their imagination can bloom. In this practice of prayer and meditation, the imagination is grown. For it is this which allows the child to understand their connection to God and Truth.

Love is elimental to growth for all children. A child that knows love, is love, expresses love, grows strong and healthy. As they grow a sense of compassion and care develops for all life.

Peter Lyons
Australia
June 2011

Children's Meditation

A Child's Lullaby

Hush a bye, don't you cry, mamma's gonna buy you a strawberry pie.
Say a prayer, take you're Teddy Bear, and fly off to fairylands and play.

Hush a bye, my little man, mamma's gonna stay with you as long as she can.
Close you're eyes and go to sleep, and join your mamma counting sheep.

And in awhile, we'll see you smile, cause you'll be happy as can be.
So hush a bye, don't you cry, mamma's going to stay with you awhile

Hush a bye, my little man, mamma's gonna buy you a choo-choo train.
And if it runs off the track, mamma's gonna put it back again.

And if some night you wake in fright, you're mamma will always be there.
To tell you tales of ships with sales, or the man in the store,
Who fell through the floor and lots more, and lots, lots more,
Cause that's what you're mums for.

Children's Meditation

Hush a bye, don't you cry, mamma's gonna buy you a strawberry pie.
Say a prayer, take you're Teddy Bear, and fly off to fairylands and play.

Maybe we should develop a Crayola bomb as our next secret weapon, a happiness weapon, a beauty bomb. And every time a crisis developed, we would launch one. It would explode high in the air - explode softly - and send thousands, millions, of little parachutes into the air, all floating down to earth, boxes of Crayolas. And we wouldn't go cheap, either - not little boxes of eight. Boxes of sixty-four, with the sharpener built right in. With silver and gold and copper, magenta and peach and lime, amber and umber and all the rest. And people would smile and get a little funny look on their faces and cover the world with imagination.

~Robert Fulghum ~

Children Are Special People

The innocence of children has always intrigued me. I never ceased to be amaze by how children can show us, contrary to some opinions, a personality long before we have had a chance to influence them. I first noticed this as the eldest of a family of nine children, as each of my younger siblings began to walk and talk. We all had the same parents, and the same influences in those early days, yet we all developed totally different interests and personalities to our parents and our siblings.

It wasn't long before I was convinced that we knew more at that age than we could possibly have learned from what our parents or other members of the family had taught us in that short time. Yet as adults, we assume we are the superior intelligence, and often dismiss this individuality expressed by children, simply as an idiosyncrasy that a child will grow out of. It is my belief that this individuality is the pure spirit of the child who, so far in its current physical life, hasn't been conditioned by the natural interferences of the world in which we all participate.

I believe it is a wise idea that parents keep a record of their child's differences, particularly in the case where parents have more than one child. Not just to record their cute little eccentricity that can have them entertaining and surprising us, but also the level and quality of knowledge they display before attending pre school or the first few years of their school life.

Those that have kept these records with an open mind, soon come to the realization that their little ones are more than just offspring of their parents. Individuals open to reincarnation are most inclined to see the obvious: Their child has been here before.

An instance in Hervey Bay strongly enforced this for me when my friend's daughter gave me a lecture in baby talk that totally shocked us all. The child was about two, and still in nappies (diapers). A group of us, including the child's parents, had met for a meditation, and we were in a very relaxed mood, discussing certain matters, when someone asked me a question of a psychic nature.

I immediately went into my meditative state and asked for an answer. That was when this little one, more an adult than a child, in no uncertain terms gave me a verbal bashing. I didn't have a clue what she had said, nor did her mother, but it was obvious that she disapproved of my psychic interaction.

Obviously we were all shocked and humoured by this little one's outburst. Was this a reflection of a previous belief that she brought over from a past life? I guess we will never know.

Sadly, most parents see their children as reflections of either their partner or his or her family, or of their own family, which they link the idiosyncratic habits of the child back to. The child, who reflects the interests or the wishes of a particular parent, tend to be seen as carrying the genes of that family.

With the belief of reincarnation, there is an understanding that the soul of the child has already collected many habits, mannerisms, and shortcoming from previous incarnations. These may not necessarily come from current family members in this life. These mannerisms tend to stay with the child for around the first fifteen years of their new life. Apparently those mannerisms and traits, carried over past life memories, tend to effect this life time. It appears that the collected habits and mannerisms from past life memories are easier to view in those first years of life.

Contrary to some points of view, we are not here to be punished for past deeds, or to pay retribution for wrongs done to others. In the process of experiencing all there is to experience life after life, the purpose of us returning to past weaknesses to deal with in different scenarios is what motivates us onward and upward from life to life.

The whole purpose of this return process is to draw the soul closer to its Creator by facing obstacles, jumping hurdles and experiencing every conceivable experience from life to life, in a physical form, till there are no experiences left for that soul to undertake.

We are extensions of the Creator, or the manifestation. We are the Creator's coalface workers, or hands. For us to blame ourselves for how others have harmed or hurt us, is as silly as hands complaining because the get damaged as a result of the owner's involvement in servile work.

A family member, concerned because her son was convinced he was going to die on his 18 birthday, asked if I could reassure her and her son, that this would not happen. I said though I could see some sadness and a shock occurring around that time, I couldn't see anything bad happening to him. It was some months after the event that she told me what had happened.

Convinced he would die, and not wanting it decided by fate, he organised the most dangerous of activities for that day. He booked a skydiving session with an established skydiving company. On the morning he was to have jumped, he woke with a serious stomach virus and so cancelled the day's activity, opting instead to spending the rest of the day in bed. The next day he heard that the woman he was to have jumped with had decided to jump alone.

She was an experienced jumper with many hours behind her. As she left the plane a wind gust entangled her parachute and she and the knotted chute plummeted to the ground. She didn't survive the fall. Was this a psychic experience encountered by my relative, or an event that had occurred in a past life around

the same time as this occurrence? I don't know, other than there was a huge change in this young man's life from that time on.

Children's Meditation

Another case of the possible carrying over of a past life was when another family member, as a young boy, displayed slow, clumsy and deliberate motor skills.

As he began to first walk, he would hesitate when asked to do some particular chore, action or skill. When he did finally get motivated, it was like his body was getting a delayed signal from his brain's command. As he matured, those aspects completely left him and his life this time round has been excellent for him. Fortune, opportunities, ease and good luck seem to constantly befall him now. My Guides told me he was seriously disabled in his past life and was possibly afflicted with Cerebral Palsy.

Interestingly enough, he worked for the earlier part of his adult life with intellectually and developmentally disabled people and his best friend has Cerebral Palsy. His interest and career is based on all things physical with a bent for the outdoors. This is something he would have been totally denied in that past life.

Children are very creative and free from birth through middle school, as the hormones surge through their bodies they become more aware of earthly attachments. During this time they must face their own mortality. In doing so great fear and joy seem to go hand in hand. It is by our diligent attention to the care of their souls that they grow to become caring and compassionate adults.

We do not need to awaken the soul in a child it is already there. We only need to help them to learn to use their senses and mind so that they may understand they are the living incarnation of their soul. Each child's journey is different and full of potential. No one can predict a life. We can only help our children to prepare for life in such a way to help them find meaning and purpose.

All children are conceived in love, from the Spiritual perspective, not necessarily in all physical instances. They are the embodiment of absolute love. Only through practice of accepting of their true nature can they hold it dear to themselves. A child is the expression of the soul. It is through the creative use of their mind and senses that they come to embrace this reality.

Children may well have personalities derived from either parent's genes. However, it is their soul that eventually determines how these little creatures will develop in this particular incarnation. Contrary to the belief of some, children are our responsibility, not our possession. As much as they are not open vessels waiting for our academic system or us to fill them with wisdom, neither should they be free to do as they wish.

We live in a society with rules and regulations, developed over centuries, which aims to serve the current and future generations. If that generation's members wish to make appropriate changes to the system and laws, assuming they live in a free country, they can do so via legal means.

In order that sensible and advantageous rules are made for the good of all of our society, the majority of the community need to make informed choices. Hence why we need to impart and encourage the use of discernment and balance with our children from a very early age. Encouraging the child to develop a moral conscience basis does this best.

This also encourages self-discipline, self-control and self-esteem, knowing that they have taken some steps to inform themselves before making any important decisions. In fact if we look at our children with an open mind, we will see they are as much our teachers as we are theirs, and often with wisdom beyond their years.

We can learn much by listen to their opinion and point of view, without an automatic assumption that they can't possibly know as much as us. Again this is because they have brought over a fair amount of accumulated knowledge from their past lives, even if they aren't conscious of it. That is not to say that we totally entertain everything the child says or requests. Quite the contrary, we are their sounding board.

What we agree or disagree to needs to be based more on societal norms, rather than personal opinions, or at least the difference needs to be explained to them. We need to be conscious of the possibility of sending mixed messages to our children when we use the words no and yes.

To say no, only to have their repeated request change our mind, simply because to do so stops them nagging, only teaches the child that the no word can be manipulated.

Again the reason we are taking this approach is not to be unkind to our children, but to prepare them for what society expects, and will enforce upon them, particularly in their adult life.

The child that has learned to manipulate a parent's correction might find themselves before a magistrate on all sorts of charges, simply because they weren't shown how to respect authority.

Children's Meditation

To speak truly, few adult persons can see nature. Most persons do not see the sun. At least they have a very superficial seeing. The sun illuminates only the eye of the man, but shines into the eye and heart of the child. The lover of nature is he whose inward and outward senses are still truly adjusted to each other; who has retained the spirit of infancy even into the era of manhood.

~Ralph Waldo Emerson ~

Discipline

I have had some parents balk at the use of the word discipline, particularly those of us who were captives to a form of cruelty that wrongly carried the same name, once considered the norm prior to the revolution of the sixties and seventies.

True discipline encourages the child to be at peace within, a discipline that builds absolutes that this child knows are appropriate and inappropriate according to their own personal values, not values forced on them that they might abhor.

A true discipline is one where the child gains an understanding of what is right, pure, true and good, before they reach adulthood. This then gives them an informed and independent value system, or their own morals and conscience bases, on which to determine how best to interact with society's values and laws.

A good parent knows that the parameters, which they use to determine right and wrong for their child, should be the same as those they use for themselves. This kind of parenting encourages consciousness of why correction is necessary by avoiding complicated and contradictory, and mostly unnecessary, frivolous rules.

As a good parent we give confidence to our children's self-empowerment and self-determination by encouraging them to build their own moral conscious base, and we only have around fifteen to eighteen years in which to do so.

After that, they are exposed to the many and varied opinions and values, which we all faced as we mature. How well they have entrenched their own values will determine how well those values withstand any opposing force.

If, as a parent, you are following the rules of Truth, as you understand them, it is most likely that your children will develop similar values, expressed in their own way. By observing our child's interpretation of our imparting, we get to learn more about how they, and others see us. Children are very special people, and often have much to teach us.

Children's Meditation

The Weekend Machine

The piston is rat shite, the rings don't exist
And the noise would drive anyone sane round the twist.
The fuel tank leaks petrol, the carbie leaks air:
This machine would drive most people into despair.

But come Friday arvo (afternoon) any time from half three, no matter the weather or mum's stern decree,
This young man of stamina and youthful ideals
Risks body and soul on his tin can on wheels

First comes the ritual, perform it he must; A cup full of gas down the carbie (carburetor) to blast
The old girl into action – at least that's his claim,
Then its pump on the starter until he goes lame

Finally after an hour or so, he gets his obstinate baby to go With a belch of blue smoke, followed by a large flame, And indecent language as he snaps the drive chain

A scream from the kitchen, "Son turn off that din.
Wash up and clean up, it's time to come in."
But she might as well whistle or go fly a kite
Than try get her son away from his bike.

With chain fixed, a rev and a honk on the horn
And one or two wheel spins around the back lawn

Children's Meditation

And with oily smoke showing the motor is ill
He guns it towards the distant blue hills,
It's 9 p.m. and her son's not come back.
Mum's heads her old buggy out on the back track,
With spotlight and rough roads and back giving pain,
She swears her son won't go biking again.

A yell from the darkness, "Hey mum, over here.
The thing's shot itself, its shattered a gear,
Or maybe it's got a leg out of bed."
Put simply folks, his old bike is dead.

Thrown unceremoniously up on the back,
They both return home down the old narrow track.
They travel in silence for neither feels well;
The son's lost a loved one and mum's back is hell.

Saturday morning, it's quarter to nine,
Mum thinks her son is out of his mind,
For he's out in the back yard - parts strewn round.
He started 'fore breakfast and stripped the bike down.

She looses her temper; can't take any more.
She tried sleeping last night flat on the floor,
But that only made her back pain grow worse,
"This junk's for the tip son, the Ute's (small Australian truck) now a hearse."

It's quite in the neighbourhood now the bike's gone;
Though the campaign is strong to buy a new one,
He's still time to kill 'fore he turns seventeen
When he knows mum will buy him his next dream machine.

Peace in a Child's Soul — Peter Lyons

Children's Meditation

Grown-ups never understand anything for themselves, and it is tiresome for children to be always and forever explaining things to them.

~Saint-Exupéry, *The Little Prince*, 1943~

Indigo Children

There has been a lot of talk concerning the sudden discovery of the Indigo Child. These Indigo Children were seen as special and different. The claim was that these highly intuitive, if somewhat hyperactive super children, had began to arrive among us beginning in the nineteen seventies.

Their aim and purpose was to lead us into the new age with a totally different process of thinking. It was claimed that peace, love and non-violent communal living were their standards.

The bulk of the Indigo Children would have been in their early to mid twenties in 2003, which leaves one wonders where these super children, and their particular pursuit of brilliance, went during the escalation of violence and contrivance of wars, such that we've had since 2001.

In actual fact this new generation including these Indigo Children appear to be more selfish and far less comunally oriented than their predecessors.

There is nothing wrong with the concept of Indigo chil

dren, so long as we understand that we are all potentially children of peace, either in the making, or were so in past lives.

Therefore we are all potentially Indigo children.

All children are potential leaders in some field of expertise, and all children are as good as the teachings and nurturing they receive, both externally and intuitively. There certainly have been some very special children who have come into existence in all generations, for as long as we have been reincarnating.

However, it is the generation, or the collective consciousness of the majority of that time which encourages or discourages peace, not the individual.

Mother Therese wasn't an exception. She was the reflection of a projected intention within that generation that came from years of oppression and violence in the world culminating into two major wars and numerous minor ones.

This generation strove to change the anomalies of the anti peace mentality that dominated the world. It seems we live in a time where freedom to express diversity of opinion is castigated into silence by the minority of those in authoritarian positions. It is during this kind of silencing we are most likely to see the expression of truth rise from the masses and true peace emerge.

Children's Meditation

And sadly it is during this time of peace, contentment and good will that we are most likely to see the build up of the bully and the aggressor who then brings forth a time of war and aggression again.

There are no magical cures for the world, no easy solutions, and no super children being born at a specific time to save us, anymore than there are super aliens preparing to lift us off this disintegrating planet on which we currently abode.

To claim certain children have been born at this specific period in history to bring us into this brave new world is not unlike Hitler's claim concerning the Arian youth of his time. It is our consistency and determination to want the Power of Peace manifested in the physical world, as it is in the spiritual world, which will bring the peace we crave. In other words, it is the dedication of soul energy, as opposed to the collective of a physical society, which will bring about an everlasting peace.

Or if I could be permitted to re write part of the Lords Pray, "May the Kingdom of Peace and Truth come, and It's will be done, here in every one of us, as well as in our material world."

Prayer and Meditation

Praying or meditating alone won't change very much. It is the state of mind of the participants that determines if the prayer or the meditation will achieve anything of value. To try encouraging peace meditations, or prayers within our children or ourselves, when there are unresolved issues on their or our minds, defeats the purpose.

The unresolved matters must be addressed first, before we can look at entering this still place in our mind where Peace reigns. Anyone who has been involved in group meditations, or psychic circles will know that unless the participants are of oneness of purpose or of mind, the peace sough is less than expected.

The way we live our life determines the level of peace we can achieve in our day-to-day living, a topic I have covered in much detail in my previous work On The Light Path, A Psychic's Journey.

Children's Meditation

Saturday Morning

It's Saturday morning and I'm ten years old,
I grab my bait, my fishing pole
And head down the river to laze my days away

The morning bird sings a simple song
As I watch the river roll along,
There's no other place that I would rather be.

And I feel so high, I feel like an eagle in flight,
Or like a seagull winging across the sea.

Yes I feel so high—I'm high in the sky.
I have sunny blue skies and wings to set me free.

I bait a hook and throw in a line,
Catch a Flathead, I'm doing fine,
There's nothing like having some
fresh cooked fish for tea.

I lie on my back and enjoy the sun,
If this is work then it sure is fun.
And mum and dad will be so pleased with me.

Yes I'm flying high, just like an eagle in flight,
Or a seagull winging across the sea

Yes I'm flying high—high in the sky.
And I don't need blue skies or wings to set me free.

An angel can illuminate the thought and mind of man by strengthening the power of vision.

~St Thomas Aquinas~

The Starting Point

Children need to connect to Inner Peace as much as adults. For some it may be family prayer, as was my childhood. For others it may be meditation, or simply a time where all family members still their minds from the turmoils of the word.

Of course sitting by a peaceful stream, throwing in a line and whiling the day away is possibly the best for older children who have the luxury of finding such a deserted place these days. Whatever the method the earlier such relaxation methods are started in the child's life the better.

Not so much to remove or prevent interference, but to encourage peaceful intimacy between their invisible friends, fairies, guardian angels or guides and themselves. Who better to distract them away from danger than their own personal guardians?

I mentioned earlier of the young nappy clad child giving me an ear bashing in baby talk. A few years later, her mother was explaining meditations to her, as a means of interacting with angels. In a matter of fact statement this young daughter said, "Well you know

Fairies are baby angels, don't you mum." The more we encourage our children to interact with their guardian angels or guides, the more likely they are to turn to them at times when we may not necessarily be available.

I was visited by a young woman who had lost both her parents in a head on car accident in Victoria, when she was twelve. She said her mom, who used to regularly meditate, had said that if anything should ever happen to her, or her father, they would come back to her in meditations. It was a standard practice for the whole family, which included her older brother, to have a family meditation prior to them going to bed. This happened up until the parents were killed.

When she first heard of the death of her parents, she said she was grief stricken to the point of almost being comatose. A few months later her brother and an aunt started to do the meditations, as a form of remembrance. She said it was like the essence of her parents was right there in the circle, returning them to the serenity as it was when they had all participated back in that earlier and happier time.

She said that even the psychiatrist, who had been dealing with her before this, was quite amazed at her recovery. In the session she had with me, I could feel her surrounded by a very high level of guidance. This guidance had been her protection since her parent's passing. However, I felt her parents had long passed onto a higher realm and I had qualms about telling her so.

Children's Meditation

I knew I couldn't keep anything back that I was given, so with much reluctance I passed this information onto her. She smiled and said it was one of the first things she and her brother had been told by their angels not long after their parent's passing. She said they were a little sad when they were first told, but then in time, understood this process protected them from negative energies masquerading as their parents.

As a Catholic family, my parents and my siblings routinely participated in the Family Rosary, and to a lesser degree, the Mantra known as the Litany. This custom became so central to our lives that all other family activities were built round it. It not only brought the family together in prayer, it also encouraged a routine period where silence and serenity had a priority in the family.

It often served to put to sleep the younger members of the family at an appropriate time. The category of reflection you adopt for your child depends on what is appropriate for you and your belief. If you are religious, and you find the child responds well to prayer, then that is the area you should look into.

If your child does not settle well to silence or chanting, then music may well be the answer. And of course, those that feel a meditation is appropriate then obviously that form of quiet time is the answer.

Peace in a Child's Soul — Peter Lyons

Fluffy Town

I'm heading out to Fluffy Town,
And there a child I'll be
Deep in the forest, set back in the hills
Where I feel safe and free

Fish in the stream there never fear harm,
The gardens are always green.
Children and old folks sit down by a lake
Sharing each other's dreams.

Come into this peace, this calm
Throw off your chains, be free
Leave behind your hurts your qualms
Open your spirit and be
Let it be

There's a place I love called Fluffy Town,
Where my inner child run's free
Deep in the forest, set back in the hills,
That only I can see

Every child is an artist. The problem is how to remain an artist once he grows up.

~Pablo Picasso~

A Children's Meditation

For those that would like to participate with their child in an imaginary based meditation, then this may well be for you. It is a meditation I was given by spirit for children and older children (adults) alike, and who doesn't want to be a child again?

Feel free to adapt it suit your circumstance. To start, the environment needs to be distraction free. Restlessness or uncomfortable positioning will only distract from the peaceful state you're trying to encourage, so that needs to be addressed before commencing. Water features, incense, or music are a good idea also, assuming they are appropriated to the mood.

Playing soft mood music is best recommended, so long as it relates to a state of peace and not a song that may link back to an activity that could easily cause disruption. As with all meditations, the child needs to relax their breathing. Slowly breathe in, hold the breath without straining, and then releasing the breath is the best way to start this.

Initially the child may exaggerate the action, but in time, as they familiarise themselves with the exercise, they will proceed in an acceptable manner.

Now it is time to use their imagination.

Suggest to the child that they are now flying through the clouds as safe as safe can be, like Peter Pan or a similar character that they know. As they tip their right arm, they fly to the right. As they tip their left arm, they fly to the left.

You could encourage them in their mind to create a Superman action with their hands together. Pointing their hands upwards as they zoom up, and pointing down as they zoom down. It is not advised that the child be encouraged to actually move their hands, as this will distract from the imagery and depth of meditation. The best idea, in such a situation, is to remind the child that this is an exercise for their mind, not their physical body, and that one must be still in order that the other is achieved.

Concentrating on the flying process in the early stages is to encourage a feeling of safety as well as imagination while meditating. As the clouds start to clear, out in the distance, they can see a wonderful castle on top of a hill. There are waterfalls around the mountains and the mountains are covered in snow.

There are rivers and lakes below, and huge trees of all sizes in the forest, but there are no dangerous animals, only happy and pleasant ones. As they get closer to the castle, they can hear loud clapping and shouts of joy. They can see millions and millions of fairies of all sizes, all around the castle, some flying, some sitting on the roofs of buildings, and some on the balconies.

They are all shouting a welcome and clapping because your child is coming home to their castle. This is your child's own personal and magical place.

And as your child lands on the roadway leading to the castle, a huge drawbridge is lowered down from the entrance, allowing your child to enter over the moat-like creek running below. Only your child can enter this sacred place, though every one of us has our own. All their baby angels, in the form of fairies, come out to welcome your child, and carry him or her into this very beautiful castle. As they enter, these baby angles take away all the hurts, worries, sadness and pains of your child's day. So now, as your child enters this magnificent place, they enter without any unhappy thoughts or memories whatsoever.

It may take a few attempts for some children, especially beginners, to get to this level, but remember it is the repetition of a meditation, not the particular meditation that matters. What they may not achieve this time; they could well do next time, or the time after. Hopefully by this time, your child will have gone to sleep, or is very close.

Once they are asleep, you in your mind, can thank the child's guides on your child's behalf and then sneak out to do a meditation yourself if you so wish. Alternatively you can stay with the child and continue on from where they went to sleep. If they haven't gone to sleep at the end of the meditation, especially older children, you can encourage them to thank their guides before going to sleep. Remind them that even though the meditation is finished, their guides are still there protecting them.

Next day, for both those children that fall asleep and those that didn't, a gentle reminder of the night before is a good way to help them to link back to how they felt. This then encourages them to draw on those peaceful feelings from the meditation, and to bring them into this new day.

At those times when your child has you exasperated beyond tolerance, a reminder of how they felt at their last meditation session can, in some cases, trigger them back to the previous state of peace and giving you the serenity you desperately crave.

It is important to encourage your child to explain and express any thought that might have come to mind during or after the meditation. Never dismiss what they say as worthless, or discourage a child's dream, as there could be some gems hidden in the childish interpretations that show themselves at a later time.

You don't know what that child's life path may be, anymore than the child does at that age. A good idea is to write down, or if they are older, for them to write down what they felt, saw, or heard during the meditation, or any reflections they might mention later. An older child might enjoy keeping a meditation journal. They can write down feelings and meditations and any ideas that come to them.

Using your own imagination, and using the same basic ingredients, you can create a different meditation from time to time. It is also a good idea to encourage children to make up their own meditation where possible.

You do a particular meditation with them a couple of times through the week, and then encourage them to make up their own meditations the other nights. This also encourages their guides to expand peaceful thoughts in their minds from an early age, which in turn brings their guides closer to them.

Something In The Air

Something in the air tonight got to me,
Bought me back to yesterday,
When I would sing and I would play alone.
When I'd pretend that I'd be someone special
And dream I'd join a famous rock roll band

Dad would say that I was just a dreamer
'Music never makes you rich'
So I went and threw it all away
Changed my plans, my life path and direction
And never got to be that special star

Yet I've watched sunrise on the water,
the evening mist out on the lake
I left the frosty bitter mornings,
for a moon rising high over Hervey Bay

Something in the air tonight that's special,
I see my life has changed and
I'm back to where it all began,
I know now that I had to be that dreamer
And that I had a special role to play

Adults are obsolete children.

~Dr. Seuss~

Our Child Within

In Australian society, the male is not encouraged to participate in conversation of mixed sexes, rather he is expected to be the listener with the occasional quiet smiles or reactionary grins. Unintentionally, the child within the male is discouraged.

I have always involved myself in conversation, adding anecdotes, one-liner punch lines, and generally involving my self in both participating in conversations as well as listening.

My manner could easily be described as child like on occasions. Recently, while gathered with a group of friends and acquaintances, one person said I came across more like a child than an adult.

Though it was said in a light-hearted fashion, one didn't have to be overly sensitive to have construed it as a thinly veiled criticism. My reply was that, on observation, most people's inner child gets securely locked in a dungeon, while some serious and sometimes unpleasant possession performs sarcastic actions through that person's outer persona.

Our child within should never be seen but not heard. It

should be encouraged and allowed expression as much as possible. It is often in lovemaking or in times

of romantic interactions that we see the child perform, but then put back in the dungeon when we progress through our daily activities.

How often do we look at shopping through the eyes of our inner child? How often do we see a meal or a gathering in a similar light to the way we acted out tea parties when children? When was the last time we saw fun in a repetitive chore? When it comes to humorous encounters with friends, how many times do we instigate them? Do we look to others for our fun times, our best memories, or rewards?

Isn't it time we took our child within out for a party? One ways we can do this is to give ourselves a break from our daily routine, and do something completely different.

It may mean taking a ride on a train to the city for those that live and generally shop in the suburbs and who haven't been on a train in years or the reverse for those that live in the cities. It may be going to the nearest park on a designated day and cooking lunch at the council provided bar-b-q where such facilities exist. It may be taking time out to enjoy a movie, or shouting your self a dinner at a restaurant of choice.

You may well say that you do one or more of these things already. The question is, who is being treated, the adult you or the child you? There has to be a mental awareness that you are not simply having a time to yourself, but that you are deliberately entertaining that child-like, fun-loving aspect of yourself.

In the family environment, there could be a declaration of a particular random day as child within day. May I suggest however, that it might be in the best interest of the family's sanity, if not all members chose the same day?

If we accept it is more than appropriate to reward ourselves in such a manner, for no other reason than we need to lighten up occasionally, how natural it will be for our children to follow such examples as a matter of course. Don't children respond best to another child, even when that child is twice or three times their age?

Peace in a Child's Soul   Peter Lyons

Heading To the River

Summer morning, gonna be a scorcher,
dad's out bailing hay
Fire's blazing in the kitchen, mum is sweating away
Girls are busy in the laundry boiling dirty clothes
Boys are outside in the garden; shovel, rake and hoe
Granny's yelling from the cow bail;
cow has kicked the pail
And me I'm heading down to the river, planning on skimming stones

Uncle Jed working in the shed, trying
 to make the tractor go
His son Art, sorting out parts;
 never seen him work so slow
Aunty Jess' house is a mess;
chooks have wandered through
And Giggling Gert the local flirt
 is talking on the telephone
Everyone is flat out busy; they've got lots to do
But me I'm heading down
to the river gonna skim a stone or two

Children's Meditation

Dreaming - while others are making hay
Scheming - yeah scheming my life away
Swimming - in the cool clear mountain stream.
There's a lot to be said about
being the youngest member of the family

Sunday morning everybody's yawning
as we head off to church to pray
Nobody wants to, but everybody has to;
fearful we'll go astray
Dad and mum up front in the buggy,
the girls sit in behind
While me and my brothers are
sitting on the old mare slowly making time
They're discussing who they're gonna
take out dancing next weekend
But me I plan to head to the river
just as soon as the praying's done

Dreaming - while others are making hay
Scheming - yeah scheming my life away
Swimming - in the cool clear mountain stream.
There's a lot to be said about being the youngest member of the family

Peace in a Child's Soul — Peter Lyons

Conclusion

As the old adage goes, you're only as old as you feel, to which I add, if you entertain youthful feelings, you stay young. Of course the opposite also applies.

I am sure you have met some 'old attitude' children or young adults who seem to be ready more for a wheel chair than for their first motor vehicle. I've been blessed with very youthful older people in my life, particularly on my mother's side of the family.

The words from a song of mine above reflect my great aunt's life and her recollections as a young girl, though adjusted for rhyming purposes. Sadly however, not all seem to see the fun in youth as she did.

A few years ago, I had cause to visit a retirement village where the aged residents were in constant need of care. I was with a mother and her two children, and as we made our way down a long corridor to visit this woman's frail grandmother, we passed by a number of residents sitting in various places outside their respective rooms.

Some would spark up and smile when they saw the children; other were too frail to notice and a third cate gory, sadly in the majority, grumbled at the exuberance of their young visitors.

As is my habit, I took a closer observation of the different ones as we passed. Those that enjoyed the children, though still incapacitated, were just itching to jump out of their confines and interact with the kids.

Those that growled or frowned at the children's presence looked like they were carrying the weight of the world on their shoulders.

Of course I don't know that some of these particularly unpleasant-displaying older citizens weren't in pain, but then again the young at heart older citizens could have been in pain also.

It struck me that if we appreciate children, then we are also entertaining our own child within, and would naturally display a more exuberant nature.

I was then reminded of some parents I knew who saw their children as chores, responsibilities or burdens and who could be well on their way to developing into this grumpy kind of older person. Many of these parents were the 'what about me' kind who believed they were owed for having children.

Sadly, I pondered, this was more likely the kind of person one would find among those abandoned to old folk's homes, only to receive an occasion perfunctory visit from their children or grand children.

Just because we gave birth, or supported the birth of our children, doesn't mean that they owe us, quite the contrary.

It is in our best interest that we let these 'little people' help us rejuvenate our inner child before that authoritarian part of us takes control and eventually destroys whatever is left of our child within.

It is my belief that we need to be open to laughter, to instigating fun and open to creative mind options if we wish to live a full and enjoyable life.

We don't have control over how long we will live this particular life, but we do have control over how enjoyable it can be.

And it all starts when we encourage the Peace in Our Child's Soul.

Happy reading

Colophon

Titles set in Aspen
Text: Georgia
Fairies: WWFancy Fairy

Set with Adobe Indesign
Digitally printed in USA

Little Stars Little Moon
www.littlestarslittlemoon.com
littlestarslittlemoon@gmail.com

www.ingramcontent.com/pod-product-compliance
Lightning Source LLC
Chambersburg PA
CBHW030005050426
42451CB00006B/121